P9-DHS-015

DATE DUE

MAR 3 1 2015	

BRODART, CO.   Cat. No. 23-221

CATS SET VII

SELKIRK REX CATS

Kristin Petrie

ABDO Publishing Company

visit us at
www.abdopublishing.com

Published by ABDO Publishing Company, PO Box 398166, Minneapolis, MN 55439.
Copyright © 2014 by Abdo Consulting Group, Inc. International copyrights reserved
in all countries. No part of this book may be reproduced in any form without written
permission from the publisher. The Checkerboard Library™ is a trademark and logo of
ABDO Publishing Company.

Printed in the United States of America, North Mankato, Minnesota.
052013
092013

 PRINTED ON RECYCLED PAPER

Cover Photo: Photo by Helmi Flick
Interior Photos: Alamy pp. 15, 17, 19, 21; Photos by Helmi Flick pp. 5, 9, 11, 13;
 Thinkstock p. 7

Editors: Rochelle Baltzer, Tamara L. Britton
Art Direction: Neil Klinepier

Library of Congress Control Number: 2013932581

Cataloging-in-Publication Data

Petrie, Kristin.
 Selkirk rex cats / Kristin Petrie.
   p. cm. -- (Cats)
ISBN 978-1-61783-866-8
Includes bibliographical references and index.
1. Selkirk rex cat--Juvenile literature.   I. Title.
636.8--dc23
                                                    2013932581

CONTENTS

LIONS, TIGERS, AND CATS

Cats are loving companions. Yet, they are also very independent. Part couch potato and part hunter, cats are entertaining and intelligent.

Cats are members of the family **Felidae**. Members of this family range from the fierce lion to the gentle house cat. So despite their tame behavior, house cats retain a bit of the wild!

Wild cats entered the lives of humans nearly 3,500 years ago. Humans stored food in their communities. The food attracted **rodents**. The cats hunted the rodents and saved the food.

Humans **bred** different cats to strengthen desired qualities. This resulted in calmer, friendlier, and prettier cats. In time, the cats became household pets.

The same selective **breeding** continues today. To date, there are more than 40 breeds of **domestic** cats. One of them is the beautiful and unusual Selkirk Rex.

The Selkirk Rex cat

SELKIRK REX CATS

In 1987, Montana cat **breeder** Jeri Newman received a call from a local animal shelter. Shelter workers had a kitten with an unusual curly coat. They thought she might want the kitten.

Newman adopted the kitten. The kitten was kind of bossy. So, Newman named her Pest!

Newman was interested in cat **genetics**. Pest's curly coat and sweet personality were intriguing! Newman wondered if Pest's kittens would inherit these features. So, she bred Pest with a male Persian cat.

Pest delivered a **litter** of six kittens. Three of them had curly hair! This meant the gene for curly hair would pass from generation to generation.

Newman continued to develop the **breed**. Eventually, she could produce consistent curly-haired kittens. The **Cat Fanciers' Association** accepted the Selkirk Rex in 1992.

Pest had a tortoiseshell and white coat like this Selkirk Rex.

QUALITIES

The Selkirk Rex attracted attention with its plush and curly coat. However, it's the **breed**'s personality that quickly wins hearts.

Selkirks are loving and affectionate cats. They are tolerant of children and like to be held and cuddled. They attach themselves to one person, following that person everywhere.

These calm, quiet cats are also playful and energetic. They enjoy playing fetch and other games, especially with their favorite person. This playful nature lasts into adulthood.

Selkirks are also intelligent and can be trained and respond well to positive attention. Many believe the Selkirk acts more like a dog than a cat. Watch out though! A smart Selkirk may figure out how to open cupboards, doors, and more!

Selkirk Rex cats were named for the Selkirk Mountains. This Canadian mountain range extends south into Idaho and Montana.

COAT AND COLOR

Is that a cat in sheep's clothing? One might ask this of the Selkirk Rex! The **breed**'s plush, soft coat resembles that of a woolly sheep. The undercoat is dense with fine, curly hair. The outer coat's coarse **guard hairs** are soft to the touch.

The Selkirk Rex can have a short coat or a long coat. The short-haired Selkirk's coat is medium in length. It curls in clumps from root to tip. The long-haired Selkirk's hair curls in individual ringlets. The curls intensify around the neck and tail in both varieties.

Selkirks can be any color. White, black, blue, red, and cream are common coat colors. In addition to a wide variety in color, their coats have many possible patterns.

Some are solid with color points like the Siamese. Others have spots or stripes. Still others combine colors, such as the tortoiseshell Selkirk.

Like its coat, a Selkirk's eyes can be any color.

SIZE

The Selkirk Rex has a stocky, rectangular-shaped body. It has wide shoulders, a full chest, and big bones. Large, strong muscles provide power and **agility**. All this rests on short, stout legs and rounded paws.

With all that muscle and bone, the Selkirk is a substantial cat. Be prepared when one jumps in your lap! Males weigh 12 to 15 pounds (5 to 7 kg). Females are slightly lighter, at 10 to 12 pounds (4 to 5 kg). But, they definitely are not dainty!

The Selkirk's round head is topped with wide-set ears. The ears are broad at the base and taper to rounded tips. The Selkirk's forehead is rounded and its cheeks are full. Curly whiskers sprout from the cat's short **muzzle**. The Selkirk's eyes are large and round.

Because they are curly,
the Selkirk's whiskers
break easily.

CARE

With that thick, curly coat, you might expect the Selkirk to be high maintenance. But, the Selkirk is easy to groom. Its fine hair resists **matting**. However, it does **shed**. Combing once or twice a week removes loose hair.

Selkirks rarely need bathing. But a bath can enhance their curls. A monthly bath is sufficient for this purpose.

Grooming is a good time to trim your Selkirk's claws. This prevents scratching of furniture and people. However, cats have a natural instinct to scratch. So, provide a scratching post for your cat to scratch on.

You brush your teeth every day, right? Well, a Selkirk needs the same dental care. Regular brushing removes bacteria from the teeth.

Your veterinarian will also help keep your cat healthy. He or she can **spay** or **neuter** your Selkirk. At yearly exams, **vaccinations** and a physical exam will keep your Selkirk happy and healthy.

Cats are precise groomers, but they can't do it all by themselves!

FEEDING

Cats need a healthy diet that includes protein, **carbohydrates**, and fat. Many commercial cat foods supply an excellent source of these. They provide vitamins and minerals, too.

There are several types of food to choose from. Dry cat food is less perishable than moist food. This type of food can be left out and a cat can eat as desired. In addition, dry food can help keep teeth clean.

Some cats prefer semimoist or canned foods. These foods are easily **digested** and a good source of water. Disposal of leftover moist food can prevent your cat from eating spoiled food and becoming sick.

Cats can become tired of their food over time. For this reason, it is wise to provide a variety of

*Eating small portions and playing with toys help
keep Selkirks from gaining too much weight.*

cat foods. Slowly introducing new cat foods helps
prevent finicky eating. It also provides a wider
variety of **nutrients**. When you feed your Selkirk,
don't forget to provide plenty of fresh water!

KITTENS

After mating, a mother Selkirk is **pregnant** for about 65 days. **Litters** of three to five kittens are typical. The newborn kittens are helpless. They are blind, deaf, and completely dependent on their mother.

When they are two weeks old, the kittens begin to see and hear. After about three weeks, they begin to play and explore their surroundings.

The kittens drink their mother's milk for about six weeks. When they are about nine weeks old, their teeth begin to grow in. Then, the kittens can eat solid food.

The kittens are old enough to leave their mother between 14 and 16 weeks of age. By then, they should be accustomed to human contact.

Curly-coated kittens can be born in the same litter as kittens with straight coats!

Buying a Kitten

Selkirks are very social cats. They need a lot of attention. And, owning a cat can be expensive. There is also work to be done. **Litter boxes** must be cleaned. Teeth must be brushed.

Have you decided that you are responsible enough to adopt a Selkirk? That's great! Now, you must choose between a kitten and a grown cat.

Kittens are adorable and fun. But, they come with uncertainties such as what their temperament will be as an adult. An adult Selkirk's disposition can be seen. And, adults require less training.

Next, look for a quality **breeder**. Reputable breeders have **vaccinated** and trained their kittens. They also provide some form of health guarantee. Choose wisely! Your Selkirk Rex will be a loving member of your family for 15 to 16 years.

In the United States, there are 74 million pet cats!

GLOSSARY

agility - the ability to move quickly and easily.

breed - a group of animals sharing the same ancestors and appearance. A breeder is a person who raises animals. Raising animals is often called breeding them.

carbohydrate (cahr-boh-HEYE-drayt) - a substance made by plants, which serves as a major class of foods for animals. Sugar and starch are examples of carbohydrates.

Cat Fanciers' Association - a group that sets the standards for judging all breeds of cats.

digest - to break down food into simpler substances the body can absorb.

domestic - tame, especially relating to animals.

Felidae (FEHL-uh-dee) - the scientific Latin name for the cat family. Members of this family are called felids. They include lions, tigers, leopards, jaguars, cougars, wildcats, lynx, cheetahs, and domestic cats.

genetics - of or relating to a branch of biology that deals with inherited features.

guard hair - one of the long, coarse hairs that protects a mammal's undercoat.

litter - all of the kittens born at one time to a mother cat.

litter box - a box filled with cat litter, which is similar to sand. Cats use litter boxes to bury their waste.

mat - to form into a tangled mass.

muzzle - an animal's nose and jaws.

neuter (NOO-tuhr) - to remove a male animal's reproductive glands.

nutrient - a substance found in food and used in the body. It promotes growth, maintenance, and repair.

pregnant - having one or more babies growing within the body.

rodent - any of several related animals that have large front teeth for gnawing. Common rodents include mice, squirrels, and beavers.

shed - to cast off hair, feathers, skin, or other coverings or parts by a natural process.

spay - to remove a female animal's reproductive organs.

vaccine (vak-SEEN) - a shot given to prevent illness or disease.

WEB SITES

To learn more about Selkirk Rex cats, visit ABDO Publishing Company online. Web sites about Selkirk Rex cats are featured on our Book Links page. These links are routinely monitored and updated to provide the most current information available.
www.abdopublishing.com

INDEX